BUDAPEST

It has often been said that few other capital cities of Europe have been graced with such a favourable geographic setting as Budapest. The city can boast a major waterway, the Danube bustling with ships, whose majestic flow divides the city, which on one side is dotted with hills.

The city abounds in hot springs which have for centuries fed the popular thermal baths. Budapest has indeed much to thank for its favourable location, but neither should it be forgotten that this central location played a key role in the city's stormy and turbulent history, in the course of which it was ravaged so oft and so heavily that again and again it had to be rebuilt anew.

In the first century B.C. a proud and flourishing Roman town with magnificent palaces and temples adorned with breathtakingly beautiful mosaics – still to be seen at Aquincum – arose beside the military fort built for the protection of the *limes,* which all but vanished after being literally razed to the ground by the barbaric devastations of the Migration period. Then came the Middle Ages, the next period of splendour. The Magyar tribes were strongly attracted to the rich and fertile lands of Pannonia, where they chose to settle in 896. One thousand years ago our first king, Stephen linked the country to western civilisation by imposing Christianity on his pagan kinsmen. He encouraged the erection of churches throughout Hungary and built one himself over the Roman wall remains scattered along the Danube. These edifices also vanished without a trace following the whirlwind invasion of the Mongolian hordes in 1242. In order to prevent similar ravages King Béla IV began the construction of a strong fortifications system, and chose Castle Hill as the most suitable site. By 1255 the palace serving as the royal residence and the main church were finished. There followed a period of spectacular fourishing in Buda, as well as in Pest on the opposite bank of the Danube and, slightly later, also in Old Buda. This period of splendour reached its peak in 1410 when King Sigismund was crowned German–Roman emperor and erected a Gothic palace befitting the royal residence of the imperial capital of Europe in place of the old one.

The legendary King Matthias (1458–1490), a sovereign of great erudition and profound vision sought out Italian architects to enlarge the Palace in the Renaissance style. The fame of his unparalleled library of illuminated manuscripts and of the lively cultural life at his court too enhanced the reputation and high ranking of Buda amongst the capitals of Europe. Waht remained of this welath, of this culture and of this splendour? It vanished as if it had never existed following the epic siege of 1686 which toppled the 150 years long Turkish occupation. Aside from a few surviving Turkish baths under Castle Hill, there remained nothing but ruins and rubble. The devastations were extensive in Pest and Old Buda as well. The once flourishing and proud city revived but slowly and painfully, and once it was again populated, little remained of its welath and fame for its inhabitants eked out a humble, almost provincial life. Buda was no longer a royal residence, its noblemen had long fled elsewhere and there remained no wealthy men to commision luxurious buildings, the only notable exception being the Church which, in an attempt to regain its power lost to the Reformation, launched an extensive building programme. Churches, schools and monasteries were erected in rapid succession. The breakthrough came in the 18th century when in the city scholarly life was gradually revived.

Budapest received its present-day appearance in the 19th century when Pest definitively assumed a leading role. The barely 30,000 strong city underwent a period of spectacular and brisk development, and by the mid-19th century its population doubled and redoubled. The city walls were demolished to accomodate the offices of the administrative bodies of the state, various commercial and cultural centres, as well as apartment houses were built. Monumental, but well-proportioned Classicist buildings such as the National Museum and Calvin Church were followed by edifices in the Romantic style (the Redout, the Main Synagogue, the building of the Hungarian Academy of Sciences). Following the unification of the three city parts in 1873, the city again bustled with life in preparation for the millenary celebration. The monumental public buildings of the period followed the popular Eclectic style. This explains our Gothic Parliament, a host of Romanesque bastions, a Renaissance State Opera House, a Baroque City Library and a Granadian cinema. The early 20th century saw the rise of breathtakingly beautiful Art Nouveau buildings. This architectural growth came to an abrupt halt after the First and the Second World Wars, when the city again met its doom.

This, then is our city's turbulent and stormy history explaining its peculiar architectural splendour, and visitors who wish to feel the city's unique atmosphere must bear in mind the fateful past.

...op Gellért. On a side
...nonument to the Chris-
... Stephen, who accord-
... nailed into a barrow a
...hill named after him.

Statue von Bischof Gellért. Das
Denkmal stellt den ersten christlichen
Bischof König Stephans dar, von heidni-
schen Magyaren in einem Faß von dem
später nach ihm benannten Berg in die
Donau gestürzt wurde.

La statua del vescovo Gellért.
monumento rende omaggio al vesco...
cristiano di re Santo Stefano. Secondo...
leggenda, gli antichi magiari pagani...
fecero precipitare, dal monte che po...
il suo nome in una botte irta di chio...

BUDAPEST

Viele behaupten, daß es in Europa keine zweite Metropole mit so günstiger geographischer Lage gibt wie Budapest. Budapest hat einen Strom, der zur Schiffahrt und zu Wassersporten geeignet ist, die Donau, die die Stadt fast genau in der Mitte zweiteilt. Budapest hat Berge und Thermalquellen, die die bekannten Heil- und Kurbäder versorgen. Es ist zwar wahr, daß Budapest seiner günstigen Lage recht viel verdanken kann, es darf aber auch nicht vergessen werden, daß eben diese zentrale Lage für die stürmische Geschichte der Stadt mitverantwortlich ist. Die Stadt wurde immer aufs neue zerstört und verwüstet, so mußte sie aus Schutt und Asche immer neu aufgebaut werden.

Rund um jedes Castrum entlang des Limes entstanden im ersten Jahrhundert u. Z. stolze römische Bürgerstädte mit prunkvollen Palästen, Tempeln und auch heute einzigartigen Mosaiken – als Beweis sei Aquincum erwähnt –, alle wurden aber während der Völkerwanderung zerstört. Pannoniens fruchtbarer Boden zog die ungarischen Stämme an, die sich im Jahre 896 hier niederließen. Vor tausend Jahren bekannte sich der erste ungarische König, Stephan der Heilige, zur westlichen Kultur, indem er sich für die Chirstianisierung seines Landes entschied. Überall, so auch auf den römischen Grundmauern an der Donau, wurden Gotteshäuser errichtet. Auch diese Bauten verschwanden spurlos infolge der Verwüstungen der Mongolen 1242. Um jedweder Wiederholung derartiger Zerstörungen vorzubeugen, ordnete König Béla IV. an, ein Verteidigungssystem auszubauen, wofür er das Gebiet der heutigen Budaer Burg am geeignetsten hielt. Schon 1255 stand die Burg mit Königsresidenz und Kirche. Eine nie geahnte Blütezeit begann für Buda, dem sich am gegenüberliegenden Donauufer erstreckenden Pest und, wenn auch etwas langsamer, für Óbuda. Der Aufschwung steigerte sich auch zur Zeit des 1410 zum deutsch–römischen Kaiser gekrönten Sigismund, der sich für seinen kaiserlichen Hof einen der Hauptstadt Europas würdigen gotischen Palast auf dem Budaer Burgberg errichten ließ.

König Matthias (1458–1490), Humanist und begabter Politiker zugleich, ließ Baumeister aus Italien kommen, die seine Renaissance-Bauten durchführten. Die einzigartige königliche Bibliothek und die kulturelle Atmosphäre am Hof steigerten den sowieso hohen Rang von Buda unter den Hauptstädten Europas. Was geschah mit all dem Reichtum, Prunk und Kultur? Nach der Befreiung Budas von der 150jährigen türkischen Besetzung 1686 verschwanden sie, als hätte es sie gar nicht gegeben. Von den wenigen erhalten gebliebenen türkischen Bädern am Fuße des Burgberges abgesehen blieben nur Ruinen zurück. Die Verwüstung verschonte auch Pest und Óbuda nicht. Die einst stolze Stadt rappelte sich nur langsam auf. Als die Region wieder besiedelt war, lebten und bauten die Menschen bescheiden und provinziell. Es war kein Wunder, Buda war keine königliche Residenz mehr, der Hochadel war verschwunden, niemand erteilte Bauaufträge. Die einzige Ausnahme war wohl die Kirche, die sich, um die von der Reformation entrissene Macht zurückzuerobern, in umfangreiche Bauvorhaben stürzte. Sie ließ Kirchen, Schulen und Klöster bauen. Erst im 18. Jh. trat eine Änderung ein, als sich die Behörden und die Repräsentanten der Wissenschaft erneut in der Stadt etablierten. Das gegenwärtige Antlitz von Budapest wurde im 19. Jh. geprägt, als Pest die Führungsposition endgültig übernahm. Die Stadt mit knapp 30 000 Einwohnern erlebte einen bis dahin nie gekannten Aufschwung, bis Mitte des Jahzhunderts war die Einwohnerzahl auf über 120 000 gestiegen. Die Stadtmauern wurden abgerissen, Behörden und Landesämter, Handels- und Kulturzentren, Miets-häuser schossen wie Pilze aus dem Boden hervor. Den monumental schlichten, harmonisch klassizisti-schen Gebäuden (Nationalmuseum, reformierte Kirche am Kalvin-Platz) folgten die von der Romantik geprägten Bauten wie die Pester Redoute, die Große Synagoge und die Ungarische Akademie der Wisenschaften. Nach der Vereinigung der drei Städte Pest, Buda und Óbuda zu Budapest (1873) erlebte die ungarische Hauptstadt, die sich auf das Millennium des ungarischen Staates vorbereitete, eine Blütezeit, wie sie der Stadt seit Sigismund und Matthias nicht mehr beschieden worden war. Es waren die Jahre, als die monumentalsten öffentlichen Einrichtungen im Zeichen des Eklektizismus enstanden. Deshalb besitzen die Budapester ein gotisches Parlament, romanische Basteimauern, eine Staatsoper im Stil der Renaissance oder die barocke Ervin Szabó Bibliothek. Der Aufschwung hielt auch in den frühen Jahren des 20. Jh. an, als die in Europa einzigartigen, damals umstrittenen Jugendstilbauten entstanden. Die Stadtentwicklung wurde durch den ersten Weltkrieg unterbrochen und vom zweiten Weltkrieg endgültig beendet. Das Schicksal erreichte Budapest wieder, zu Kriegsen-de lag es in Schutt und Asche. Das war also die unruhige Vergangenheit der ungarischen Hauptstadt. Sie bestimmt das eigenartige Weichbild der Stadt. Diese Vergangenheit sollte auch der Besucher verstehen, und die einzigartige Atmosphäre der Stadt empfinden. Dabei möchte Ihnen, werte Leserin, werter Leser, unser Buch behilflich sein.

 The facade of an Art Nouveau building (Martinelli square)

 Die Fassade eines im Jugendstil erbauten Hauses in der Innenstadt. (Martinelli-Platz)

La facciata di una casa in stile liberty nel Centro della città (Piazza Martinelli)

BUDAPEST

Molti ritengono che siano poche le capitali d'Europa che abbiano una posizione geografica tanto felice come Budapest. La metropoli ha un fiume adatto per la navigazione e per gli sport nautici, il Danubio che divide quasi al centro la città, ha delle colline di vaste dimensioni ed acque termali che sono fonti naturali dei numerosi bagni terapeutici. È vero che Budapest deve molto alla sua fortunata posizione, ma non si deve dimenticare che appunto la sua centralità è stata causa della storia tumultuosa della città, nel cui corso tante volte è rimasta distrutta da doverla ricostruire quasi sempre partendo dalle basi.

Nel primo secolo dopo Cristo, attorno alla guarnigione costruita in difesa dei limes, sorse una città romana fiera, fiorente, con bellissimi palazzi, templi e con mosaici di una bellezza tuttora impressionante – lo sta a dimostrare Aquincum –, ma tutto ciò è sparito a seguito delle barbariche distruzioni dei popoli migratori. C'è stato anche un Medioevo e non uno qualsiasi. La ricca terra di Pannonia ebbe ad attirare anche le tribù magiare che si stabilirono in questa area nell'896, e mille anni fa il nostro primo re, Santo Stefano congiunse il Paese alla cultura occidentale abbracciando il cristianesimo. Dappertutto furono costruite delle chiese, così anche presso le mura romane trovate sulla riva del Danubio. Questi edifici sparirono senza lasciare tracce dopo l'invasione mongola che irruppe con violenza devastatrice nel 1242. Per prevenire simili distruzioni, re Béla IV cominciò a far costruire un sistema di difesa, considerando più adatta a tale scopo la collina della fortezza di Buda. Nel 1255 era già pronta la fortezza con il suo palazzo, residenza reale e la chiesa di Nostra Signora. Buda cominciò a prosperare rapidamente, così pure Pest sulla riva opposta del Danubio e, anche se con un pò di ritardo, Óbuda. Questo slancio si intensificò ai tempi di re Sigismondo, eletto nel 1410 al trono del Sacro Romano Impero, il quale fece costruire per la sua corte imperiale un palazzo gotico degno della capitale d'Europa. Il nuovo palazzo affascinava i visitatori con le sue dimensioni, con la sua bellezza e con il gran numero di opere d'arte.

Le costruzioni rinascimentali fatte realizzare da maestri italiani chiamati dal leggendario Re Mattia (1458–1490) di cultura umanista, di largo orizzonte, la sua biblioteca di particolare valore, l'atmosfera culturale della sua Corte non fecero che aumentare il prestigio di Buda fra le capitali dell'Europa. Cos'è rimasto di tutta questa ricchezza, cultura, sfarzo? È sparito tutto come se non ci fosse mai stato dopo l'assedio del 1686 che pose fine ai centocinquanta anni di dominazione turca. A parte i pochi bagni turchi sopravvissuti, costruiti sotto la collina della fortezza, non rimase altro che un cumulo di rovine. La devastazione non risparmiò né Pest, né Óbuda. Difficilmente resuscitò dalle sue ceneri la città un tempo tanto orgogliosa, e quando la zona si ripopolò la gente visse, costruì modestamente. Non c'è da meravigliarsi, poiché Buda non era più sede reale, non c'era più nobiltà, e perciò neanche potenziali costruttori. L'unica eccezione era la Chiesa, la quale riconquistando il potere perduto ad opera della Riforma, intraprese grosse costruzioni. Furono costruite chiese, scuole, monasteri. Solo il XVIII secolo portò cambiamenti, allorquando pian piano si trasferirono nuovamente nella città gli uffici principali e anche la vita scientifica.

L'aspetto odierno di Budapest si consolidò nel XIX secolo, quando Pest ebbe ad assumersi, definitivamente, il ruolo dirigente. Nella città che allora contava appena 30.000 abitanti, ebbe inizio uno sviluppo dinamico e alla metà del secolo gli abitanti erano già oltre 120 mila. Le mura cittadine furono abolite e si costituirono, uno dopo l'altro uffici di competenza nazionale, centri commerciali e culturali, vennero costruite grandi case di abitazione. Ai monumentali edifici classicheggianti, di belle proporzioni (Museo Nazionale, Chiesa Calvin) fecero seguito il Ridotto, la Sinagoga, l'Accademia Ungherese delle Scienze, nate all'insegna del romanticismo. Dopo l'unificazione dei tre agglomerati, Buda, Pest e Óbuda avvenuta nel 1873, nella città che si preparava ai festeggiamenti del millenario della conquista del paese da parte delle tribù magiare, si svolgeva una vita pulsante mai vista dai tempi dei re Sigismondo e Mattia. Sono stati costruiti in quel periodo i più monumentali edifici pubblici all'insegna dell'eclettismo sempre più popolare. È così che abbiamo un Parlamento gotico, un bastione con mura romaniche, un Teatro dell'Opera rinascimentale, un cinematografo di stile granada, un biblioteca, la Szabó Ervin, barocca. Questo slancio continuò anche all'inizio di questo secolo quando furono costruiti numerosi edifici liberty, quasi unici in Europa. A tale sviluppo pose fine la prima guerra e poi, definitivamente, il secondo conflitto mondiale, durante il quale sulla città si abbattè ancora una volta la mala sorte e, dopo aspri combattimenti, Budapest fu quasi completamente rasa al suolo. Questo è stato il passato tumultuoso della nostra città; a ciò si deve la sua particolare fisionomia architettonica, ed è questo che deve comprendere chi vuole sentire la sua particolare atmosfera. È in questo senso che desideriamo esserLe di aiuto con questo volume.

THE CASTLE DISTRICT

This district is one of the most popular tourist spots in Budapest, lying on a high plateau overlooking the Danube. it was founded by King Béla IV in the 12th century with a view to defend the city. The Royal Palace lies in the south, whilst the northern part accomodated the burghers' town. Only four of the original 170 buildings in the Castle survived the bombardments of the Second World War. Great care was devoted to the accurate reconstruction of historical details in the course of renovation, to the preservation of medieval doorways and Baroque elements, as well as to erect building which harmonise with the old houses in vacant plots.

DAS BURGVIERTEL

Budapests bevorzugte touristische Attraktion erstreckt sich auf dem 1500 m langen und 500 m breiten Hügelrükken der Donau entlang, von König Béla IV. im 13. Jh. als Festung ausgebaut. Im südlichen Teil des Plateaus befand sich die königliche Residenz, im nördlichen die Bürgerstadt. Von den 170 Gebäuden der Burg blieben nach dem zweiten Weltkrieg nur vier erhalten. Bei der Restaurierung wurde auf die historische Authentizität, Konservierung der erhaltenen mittelalterlichen Hauseingänge und Barockfragmente und auch darauf geachtet, daß nur mileuverwandte Häuser in den Baulücken entstehen sollten.

IL QUARTIERE DELLA FORTEZZA

È una delle maggiori attrazioni turistiche di Budapest. Si estende sulla riva destra del Danubio su una altura lunga 1500 metri e larga 500 metri. Fu fondata nel XIII secolo da re Béla IV per scopi di difesa. Al lato meridionale si trovava il Palazzo Reale, nella parte settentrionale invece la città. Fra i 170 edifici della Fortezza, dopo la seconda guerra mondiale ne rimasero in piedi solo quattro. Durante i lavori di restauro è stata dedicata grande cura all'autenticità storica, alla presentazione dei portali medioevali e dei particolari barocchi rimasti, alla costruzione, nelle aree vuote fra le case, di edifici conformi all'ambiente.

Castle Palace and the southeastern walls. most imposing building on Castle Hill is undoubtedly former Royal Palace, originally built in the 13th cent The present-day neo-Baroque complex was planned Miklós Ybl and Alajos Hauszmann in the 19th cent It was meticulously renovated following the Seco World War.

Das Burgschloß und die südöstlichen Burgmauern. Das im 13. Jh. errichtete neobarocke Palastensemble erhielt seine gegenwärtige Form nach Entwürfen der Architekten Miklós Ybl und Alajos Hauszmann im 19. Jh. Mit der Behebung der während des zweiten Weltkrieges erlittenen Beschädigungen wurde in den fünfziger Jahre begonnen.

Il Palazzo della Fortezza e le mura a sud-est. L'edificio più imponente, del quartiere della fortezza è l'ex palazzo reale. Venne costruito nel XIII secolo ed assunse la forma attuale in base ai progetti di Miklós Ybl e di Alajos Hauszmann nel XIX secolo. Subì, durante il secondo conflitto mondiale, grossi danni a cui si è posto rimedio durante i lavori di ripristino iniziati negli anni Cinquanta.

 View of the Castle Palace from the southwest with the Mace Tower. The building first functioned as the medieval royal residence, it finally became the seat of the governor at the beginning of the 20th century. At present, it houses museums and libraries.

 Südwestliche Seitenansicht des Burgpalasmit dem Keulenturm. Das Gebäude diente im M telalter zur königlichen Residenz, Anfang des 20. Jh. z Sitz des Reichsverwesers. Seit der Rekonstruktion s kulturelle Institutionen (Museen, Bibliothek) darin tergebracht.

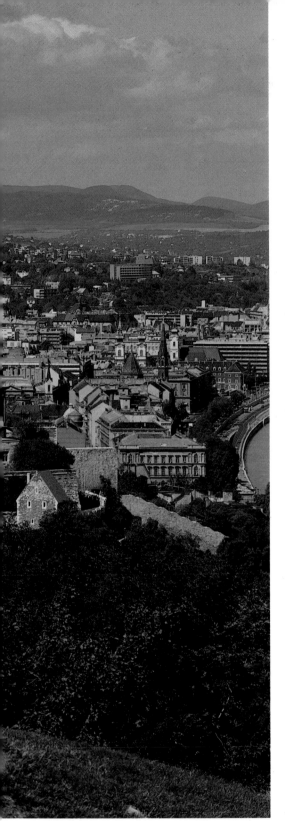

King Matthias' Fountain. This group of Art Nouveau statues sculpted by Alajos Stróbl depicts King Matthias hunting, Ilona the Fair, a maiden of legendary beauty and one of the king's falconers; it was positioned onto the wall of the palace in the course of the neo-Baroque rebuilding.

Matthiasbrunnen. Beim neobarocken Umbau des Palastes wurde die bronzene Jugendstil-Skulpturenkomposition – König Matthias als Jäger, die legendäre Schöne Ilonka und ein Falkner – von Alajos Stróbl an die Wand des Innenhofes placiert.

La fontana di Mattia. La fontana venne sistemata sul muro del palazzo nel periodo delle costruzioni neobarocche, per arricchire il cortile interno. Il complesso di statue stile liberty, realizzate in bronzo dallo scultore Alajos Stróbl, comprende le figure di Re Mattia impegnato in una battuta di caccia, della leggendaria Elena La Bella e di un falconiere.

Il Palazzo della Fortezza nel lato sud-ovest con la Torre della Clava. Nel Medioevo l'edificio funzionava come palazzo reale, all'inizio del nostro secolo era il palazzo del Reggente. Terminati i lavori di restauro ora ospita vari musei e la biblioteca nazionale.

The Castle Palace in its nightly splendour   Der Burgpalast bei nächtlicher Beleuchtung

The Cable Railway. One of the tourist attractions of Budapest is the cable railway between Chain Bridge and the Castle which has recently been restored to its original, 19th century form.

Die Standseilbahn in der Budaer Burg. Eine der Sehenswürdigkeiten Budapests ist die Standseilbahn zwischen dem Budaer Brückenkopf der Kettenbrücke und der Burg, die neulich in ihrer ursprünglichen, Form aus dem letzten Jahrhundert wiederhergestellt wurde.

La funicolare del Castello di Buda. È una delle attrattive turistiche di Budapest. La funicolare ripristinata recentemente nella sua forma originale del secolo scorso, è in funzione fra la testata, a Buda, del Ponte delle Catene e il Castello.

Il Palazzo della Fortezza illuminato

Matthias Church (Church of the Blessed Virgin; 13th–19th centuries). Built as the main church of the Castle, it served as the coronation church of Hungarian monarchs. Its present-day neo-Gothic form was planned by Frigyes Schulek (1874–96). Choral and orchestral concerts were held in the church already under King Matthias. The regularly held concerts continue this tradition.

Die Matthiaskirche (Liebfrauenkirche, 13.–19. Jh.). Die als Hauptkirche der Burg erbaute Matthiaskirche diente später als ungarische Krönungskirche und zur Türkenzeit als Moschee. Sie wurde nach Entwürfen von Frigyes Schulek im neogotischen Stil neu gestaltet (1874–1896).

La Chiesa di Mattia (La Chiesa di Nostra Signora, XIII–XIX sec.). Costruita come chiesa centrale della fortezza divenne la chiesa di incoronazione dei re d'Ungheria; durante la dominazione turca serviva da moschea. L'attuale forma neogotica si deve all'architetto Frigyes Schulek, realizzata dal 1874 al 1896. Già ai tempi di Mattia qui si tenevano delle esibizioni vocali ed orchestrali.

King St. Stephen. This 19th century statue by Ferenc Mikula standing in the southern porch depicts our first king.

 Interior of Matthias Church. The imposing neo-Gothic interior is a result of rebuildings in the last century.

König Stephan der Heilige. An der Ecke der südlichen Vorhalle der Matthiaskirche erhebt sich das im 19.Jh. von Ferenc Mikula geschaffene Reiterstandbild des ersten ungarischen Königs.

 Innenraum der Matthiaskirche. Das einheitliche imposante neogotische Kircheninterieur entstand beim Neubau am Ende des 19. Jh.

La statua di Re Santo Stefano. La statua, opera di Ferenc Mikula, realizzata nel secolo scorso, raffigura Santo Stefano, il primo re d'Ungheria.

 L'interno della Chiesa di Mattia. L'imponente interno neogotico è il risultato dei lavori di ricostruzione effettuati alla fine del secolo scorso.

 Fishermen's Bastion. One of the most characteristic buildings in Budapest, it was built between 1899–1905 according to the plans of Frigyes Schulek in a neo-Romanesque style, along the section of the fortifications walls protecting Castle Hill behind Matthias Church. Its look-out towers, terraces and corridors are reminiscent of an ambulatory.

 Die Fischersbastei. Es ist eines der charakteristischsten Bauwerke der ungarischen Hauptstadt. Es wurde zwischen 1899 und 1905 nach den Plänen von Frigyes Schulek im neoromantischen Stil als Teil der alten Burgmauern hinter der Matthiaskirche gebaut; Aussichtstürme, Terrassen und den klösterlichen Kreuzgang nachahmende Passagen.

14

Convergence of styles. The modern building of the Hilton Hotel constructed in 1976 incorporates the ruins of a medieval Dominican cloister and church – an excellent example of modern architecture fitting harmoniously into a historic setting.

Ein Rendezvous der Stile. Die Mauerreste des mittelalterlichen Dominikanerklosters und der Kirche wurden in das 1976 erbaute moderne Hotel Hilton eingegliedert; dieser Hotelbau ist beispielhaft für die Verbindung moderner Architektur und historischer Umgebung.

Incontro di vari stili. Il moderno edificio dell'Hotel Hilton è stato costruito nel 1976 con l'impiego dei muri del monastero e della chiesa medievale dei Domenicani. È un interesante esempio del nuovo criterio edilizio che colloca gli stabili in ambiente storico.

Il Bastione dei Pescatori. È una delle costruzioni più caratteristiche di Budapest. È stato edificato in base ai progetti di Frigyes Schulek, in stile neoromanico dal 1899 al 1905, nel tratto della muraglia che sta dietro la Chiesa di Mattia. È guarnito di torrette di calcare bianco, di terrazze, di galleria ad archi.

Courtyard of a house in the Castle District. An enchanting inner courtyard preserving the atmosphere of the Middle Ages inside a Baroque building with Classicist main facade, built around 1820. (Dísz square. 11)

Ein stimmungsvoller Innenhof im Burgviertel. Hier scheint noch das Mittelalter lebendig zu sein: Innenhof eines im Barockstil um 1820 errichteten Hauses mit klassizitischer Fassade. (Dísz-Platz 11.)

Corte interna dall'atmosfer storica nella Fortezza. Corte inte na di atmosfera medioevale dell'edific barocco dalla facciata classicheggian costruito attorno al 1820. (Dísz tér 1

Országház Street. A small street exhaling the atmosphere of the Middle Ages, with a recently renovated building, roofed with Zsolnay tiles, housing the State Archives in the background.

Teilansicht aus der Országház-Straße. Straße mit charakteristisch mittelalterlicher Atmosphäre, im Hintergrund das neu renovierte Gebäude des Landesarchivs mit Zsolnay-Dachziegeln.

Particolare della Via Országház. Una via dalla caratteristica atmosfera medioevale; sullo sfondo l'edificio dell'archivio dal tetto coperto di piastrelle Zsolnay, restaurato di recente.

Neo-Baroque Palace in the Castle District. The building with its lavish facade was built in 1904 and preserves medieval and Baroque remains. (Úri str. 58.)

Neobarockes Palais im Burgviertel. Das Haus mit der reich ausgestalteten Fassade wurde unter Anwendung der mittelalterlichen und barocken Mauern 1904 gebaut (Úri Straße 58.).

Palazzo neobarocco nella Fortezza. L'eidficio dalla facciata riccamente decorata risale al 1904, è stato costruito utilizzando muri medievali e barocchi. (Úri utca 58.).

ALONG THE DANUBE

Contributing to Budapest's unique atmosphere is the fact, that it is traversed by one of the largest European waterways, the Danube. In the lack of paved roads, the river became one of the main trade routes from the Roman period to the 19th century. After the great flood of 1838 which caused extensive damages in the city, the building of the embankment became a prime concern. Imposing public buildings and apartment houses were erected along the embankment, as well as modern hotels. The river is spanned by six public and two railway bridges.

AN DER DONAU

Das wohl wichtigste Kennzeichen von Budapest ist die Donau, Mitteleuropas größter Strom, der durch die ungarische Hauptstadt fließt. Schon im Pannonien der Römerzeit und bis ins 19. Jh. war die Donau – mangels entsprechender Straßen – eine der wichtigsten Handelsverbindungen des Landes. Nach dem Hochwasser im Jahre 1838, als die Stadt schwere Schäden erlitt, wurden die Ufer des Stromes aufgeschüttet und die Kaie ausgebaut. An den sicheren Ufern enstanden imposante öffentliche Gebäude und Mietshäuser, so wie heutzutage die großen Hotels. Sechs Staßen- und zwei Eisenbahnbrücken verbinden die Budapester Donauufer.

LUNGO IL DANUBIO

La caratteristica principale della fisionomia di Budapest è che la metropoli è attraversata dal più grande fiume dell'Europa Centrale, il Danubio. Dalla fine dell'epoca romana fino al XIX secolo – poiché erano poche le strade costruite – il Danubio era una delle più importanti arterie commerciali del Paese. Dopo la disastrosa alluvione del 1838 che colpì gravemente la città, si rese necessaria l'arginatura del Danubio e il rialzo del lungofiume. Sulle rive elevate sono stati costruiti imponenti edifici pubblici e case d'abitazione, ultimamente grandi alberghi. Le due rive sono collegate da otto ponti, due dei quali sono ponti ferroviari.

Budapest by night. Gellért Hill offers a splendid view of the Danube Bank.

Budapest am Abend. Das Stadtpanorama mit der Donau vom Gellértberg aus gesehen.

Budapest illuminata di sera. Dal Gellérthegy (Monte Gellért) si può godere un magnifico panorama del bellissimo Lungodanubio.

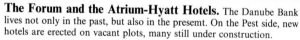

The Forum and the Atrium-Hyatt Hotels. The Danube Bank lives not only in the past, but also in the presemt. On the Pest side, new hotels are erected on vacant plots, many still under construction.

Das Hotel Forum Budapest und das Hotel Atrium-Hyatt. Das Donauufer hat nicht nur eine Vergangenheit, sondern auch eine Gegenwart. Die Baulücken am Pester Donaukorso wurden und werden auch in nächster Zukunft mit Hotelbauten geschlossen.

L'Hotel Forum e l'Hotel Atrium-Hyatt. Il Lungodanubio non ha solo passato, ha anche un presente. Nelle aree vuote fra le case, provocate dalla seconda guerra mondiale, sulla riva di Pest sono stati costruiti diversi alberghi e altri sono in programma per i prossimi anni.

Autumn comes to the Danube.
Elisabeth bridge, with Chain Bridge in the background, are perhaps two of the most remarkable bridges linking the two city parts.

Die Donau im Herbst. Die markantesten Donaubrücken sind wahrscheinlich die Elisabethbrücke und im Hintergrund die Kettenbrücke.

Il Lungodanubio in autunno. Fra i ponti che collegano le due parti della città, il Ponte Elisabetta e il Ponte delle Catene, sullo sfondo, sono forse quelli di maggior spicco.

 The Promenade. A favoured parading ground of both tourists and native citizens, the Promenade extends from Elisabeth bridge to Chain bridge, and has recently been given a face-lift.

Der Donaukorso. Am Korso am Pester Donauufer zwischen der Elisabeth- und Kettenbrücke spazieren Touristen und Budapester. Der Korso wurde in den vergangenen Jahren zu neuem Leben erweckt.

Elisabeth Bridge. The turn of the century bridge which was bombarded in 1945 was rebuilt in 1964 reusing the former piers.

Elisabethbrücke. Anstelle der 1945 gesprengten Brücke, die aus der Zeit der Jahrhundertwende stammte, wurde die neue Brücke auf den alten Brückenpfeilern als modernste Brücke der Hauptstadt 1964 wieder errichtet.

Il Ponte Elisabetta. Al posto del ponte, le cui origini risalgono alla fine del secolo scorso e bombardato nel 1945, è stato costruito nel 1964 utilizzando i vecchi pilastri il nostro ponte più moderno.

Corso Danubio. Nella parte di Pest si stende, dal ponte Elisabetta fino al Ponte delle Catene, il Corso Danubio, la passeggiata preferita dai turisti e dai budapestini; è stato rinnovato, con grande cura, in questi ultimi anni.

Water Tower on Margaret Island. Margaret Island abounds in thermal springs, and saw lavish ecclesiastic and lay building activity one of Budapest's most valuable parks. The open-air theater beside the Water Tower has regular musical performances in summer.

Wasserturm auf der Margareteninsel. Die einstige, an Thermalquellen reiche Haseninsel ist der wertvollste Budapester Park. Auf der Freilichtbühne neben dem Wasserturm finden in Sommer Musikveranstaltungen statt.

La torre idrica nell'Isola Margherita. Chiamata un tempo l'Isola delle Lepri, teatro di importanti costruzioni ecclesiastiche e civili, oggi è il più prestigioso parco di Budapest. Il teatro all'aperto nei pressi della torre idrica, ospita, in estate, grandiose rappresentazioni musicali.

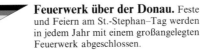

Fireworks over the Danube. The festivities of St. Stephen's day are crowned each year with impressive fireworks.

Feuerwerk über der Donau. Feste und Feiern am St.-Stephan–Tag werden in jedem Jahr mit einem großangelegten Feuerwerk abgeschlossen.

Fuochi d'artificio sul Danubio. Ogni anno, i festeggiamenti della Giornata di Re Santo Stefano terminano con magnifici fuochi d'artificio.

Chain Bridge. The first permanent bridge was completed between 1839 and 1849 after the plans of William Thierney Clark, following the unceasing organisational work of Count Széchenyi. It was one of the most modern and largest bridges of last century Europe, which is still a decisive element of the Budapest landscape.

Die Kettenbrücke. Die erste feste Brücke zwischen Buda Pest wurde dank der organisatorischen Tätigkeit István Széchenyis und nach den Plänen von William Thierney Clark 1839–1849 gebaut. Sie gehörte zu den modernsten Brücken Europas im 19. Jh. und ist ein Wahrzeichen von Budapest.

Il Ponte delle Catene. Il primo ponte stabile è stato costruito, dal 1839 al 1849, a seguito del tenace lavoro organizzativo di István Széchenyi, in base ai disegni dell'architetto William Thierney Clark. Era uno dei più moderni e più grandi ponti dell'Europa del secolo scorso ed anche oggi è fattore determinante dell' immagine della mètropoli.

 Parliament. The Parliament designed to accomodate both chambers of Parliament was built to the magnificent Neo-gothic and Ecclectic plans of Imre Steindl between 1885 and 1904. The huge mass of Parliament still reflects the representational needs and love of splendour of the country preparing its millenial celebrations. The lavish external architectural ornaments of soft limestone cannot tolerate modern polluted air and they are thus replaced by hard stone over the years.

 Das Parlament. Das Parlamentsgebäude für beide Kammern des Hohen Hauses wurde 1885–1904 nach den eklektisch-neogotischen Entwürfen von Imre Steindl errichtet. Das imposante Bauwerk widerspiegelt den Bedarf der Repräsentation und den Gefallen an Prunk des sich auf die Millenniumsfeiern der ungarischen Staatlichkeit vorbereitenden Landes. Die aus weichem Kalkstein gefertigten Skulpturen und Ornamente sind der Luftverschmutzung nicht gewachsen. Seit Jahren dauern die Restaurierungsarbeiten, wobei der Kalkstein durch härteren Stein ersetzt wird.

Il Parlamento. Il Parlamento chiamato ad accogliere le due camere dell'assemblea nazionale è stato costruito dal 1885 al 1904 secondo i progetti ecclettico-neogotici di Imre Steindl. L'immenso complesso architettonico rispecchia anche oggi fedelmente l'esigenza di rappresentanza ed il gusto per il fasto dell'Ungheria che si preparava ai festeggiamenti del Millennio. I ricchi ornamenti architettonici esteriori fatti di pietra calcarea friabile non sopportano l'aria satura di acido carbonico della nostra epoca, per cui da alcuni anni è in corso la loro sostituzione con pietra dura.

27

Interior of Parliament. The chamber of MPs seating 450 persons is still the seat of Parliament today. The former upper house now plays host to national and international congresses and meetings.

Innenraum des Parlaments. Der Sitzungssaal des Abgeordnetenhauses mit 450 Sitzplätzen ist auch heute der Sitz der Volksvertretung. Im Sitzungssaal des Oberhauses werden heutzutage ungarische und internationale Konferenzen und Tagungen veranstaltet.

▶ **Interno del Parlamento.** La sala-riunioni dei deputati che dispone di 450 posti è tuttora la sede dell'Assemblea Nazionale. La sala della Camera Alta oggigiorno ospita convegni e congressi nazionali e internazionali.

INNER CITY (Down Town)

The heart of Budapest, its administrative and shopping center, the most ancient part of the city built on the wall remnants of a former Roman fortress at a good crossing of the river Danube. Reached its peak of fame during the last century, but still guards its achieved rank. Restaurants, tea-rooms, smart shops, high class hotels along the embankment, sparkling and glittering Váci utca, Parlament, Opera House, Basilica, all offer a magnificent sight on an area bordered by Margaret and Elisabeth bridges and the Grand Boulevard.

DIE INNENSTADT

Die Budapester Innenstadt, Verwaltungs- und Einkaufszentrum, der historische Stadtkern von Pest, wurde auf den Grundmauern der römischen Festung und der günstigsten Donauüberfahrt errichtet. Die City ist von Restaurants, Konditoreien, eleganten Geschäften, anspruchsvollen Hotels am Donaukorso, der schillernden Váci Straße durchwirkt. Hier zwischen der Margareten- und der Elisabethbrücke befinden sich das Parlament, die Staatsoper, die Basilika und viele andere Sehenswürdigkeiten.

IL CENTRO DELLA CITTÀ

È il cuore, il centro amministrativo e commerciale di Budapest, l'antico nucleo di Pest, costruito sui muri della fortificazione romana creata presso il più favorevole passaggio sul Danubio. Assunse vera importanza nel secolo scorso, e da allora conserva il suo rango. Ristoranti, pasticcerie, negozi eleganti, alberghi di livello mondiale sul Lungodanubio, la smagliante Via Váci, il Parlamento, il Teatro dell'Opera, la Basilica costituiscono tutti uno spettacolo attraente in questa area racchiusa fra il Ponte Margherita, il Ponte Elisabetta e il Nagykörút.

Clotild Palaces. Designed by Frigyes Korb and Kálmán Giergl in Eclectical Art Nouveau style at the Pest entrance of Elisabeth bridge.

 Klothilde-Paläste. Am Pester Brückenkopf der Elisabethbrücke nach den Plänen von Frigyes Korb und Kálmán Giergl errichtete Jugendstilbauten.

 Palazzi Klotild. Sono opere degli architetti Frigyes Korb e Kálmán Giergl, realizzate in stile liberty presso la testata a Pest del Ponte Elisabetta.

 Redoute. Designed by Frigyes Feszl and erected on the site of the former Redoute, it perished during the fights of 1849. An unmatched splendour of European Romantic architecture. The last hundred years have seen great performances by numerous world famous artists in the concert hall.

 Die Pester Redoute. Wo die in den Kämpfen von 1849 zerstörte Redoute stand, entstand nach den Entwürfen von Frigyes Feszl das in Europa einzigartige Bauwerk romantischer Architektur: Pesti Vigadó (Pester Redoute). Im Konzertsaal traten international bekannte Künstler auf. Diese Tradition wird im kunstvoll restaurierten Gebäude fortgesetzt.

Promenade. Promenade restored to its former shape, bustling with life.

Donaukorso. Das Leben pulsiert auf dem in neues Gewand gekleideten Donaukorso.

Passeggiata sul Danubio. Sulla rinnovata passeggiata in riva al Danubio si svolge una vita assai movimentata.

Váci street. The elegant and popular shopping centre of the Inner City of Budapest.

Váci Straße. Die elegante und beliebte Fussgängerzone in der Innenstadt von Budapest.

La Via Váci. Elegante e frequentatissima via nel centro di Budapest.

Il Ridotto. Al posto dell'antico Redoute, distrutto durante i combattimenti del 1849, è stata costruita secondo i progetti di Frigyes Feszl questa opera dell'architettura romantica, quasi impareggiabile in Europa. Negli ultimi cento anni nella sala dei concerti si sono esibiti numerosi artisti di fama mondiale.

Hungarian National Museum.
Built between 1837 and 1846 to the public collection designs of Mihály Pollack for the first in the country donated by Ferenc Széchényi in 1802.

Ungarisches Nationalmuseum.
Für die erste öffentliche Sammlung, die von Ferenc Széchényi 1802 gegründet wurde, nach denn Entwürfen von Mihály Pollack 1837–1847 gebautes Museum.

Il Museo Nazionale Ungherese.
Opera dell'architetto Mihály Pollack è stato costruito dal 1837 al 1846, per accogliere la prima collezione pubblica del Paese, creata da Ferenc Széchényi nel 1802.

Academy of Sciences. A splendid neo-Renaissance building, completed between 1862 and 1865, it is a truly remarkable spot on the Danube bank. Designed for the Academy of Sciences, founded in 1825, it serves as its seat even today. Béla Bartók worked also here.

Sitz der Ungarischen Akademie der Wissenschaften. Das edle Neorenaissance-Gebäude aus den Jahren 1862–1865 prägt diesen Teil des Pester Donauufers. Für die 1825 gegründete Akademie gebaut, beherbergt es sie auch heute. Hier arbeitete auch Béla Bartók.

L'Accademia Ungherese delle Scienze. Il palazzo neorinascimentale costruito dal 1862 al 1865 è uno dei punti più caratteristici del Lungodanubio sulla riva di Pest. È stato realizzato per l'Accademia delle Scienze fondata nel 1825 e ospita tuttora tale istituzione. Ha lavorato qui anche Béla Bartók.

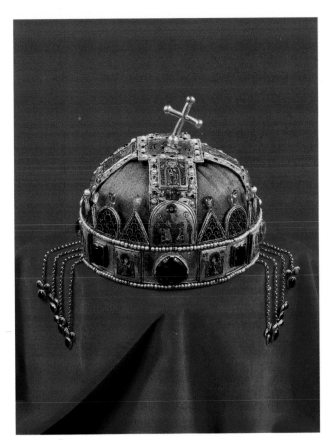

The Royal (Holy) Crown. The Crown of St Stephen is the symbol of the Hungarian nation, it was taken abroad during World War II, but since 1976 it is the most treasured item of the National Museum.

Die Heilige Krone. Die Krone König Stephans, das Symbol der ungarischen Nation, gelangte Ende des zweiten Weltkrieges ins Ausland und wurde Ungarn – und dem Nationalmuseum – erst 1976 rückerstattet.

La Sacra Corona. La corona di Re Santo Stefano è il simbolo della nazione ungherese. Durante la seconda guerra mondiale venne portata all'estero; soltanto dal 1976 è custodita gelosamente nel Museo Nazionale.

 The Opera House. The royal staircase of the Opera House

 Opernhaus. Die Königstreppe des Opernhauses.

 Il Teatro dell'Opera. Scalinata reale

Opera House. Built in neo-Renaissance style between 1875 and 1884 to the design of Miklós Ybl, the most magnificent edifice on Andrássy Avenue. Ever since its opening, it has been center of Hungarian music life.

Staatsoper. Dieser Juwel an der Budapester Andrássy-Straße wurde 1875–1884 aufgrund der Pläne des Architekten Miklós Ybl im Neorenaissance-Stil gebaut. Es ist seit der Eröffnung das Zentrum des ungarischen Musiklebens.

Il Teatro dell'Opera. Il più imponente edificio di Viale Andrássy è stato costruito fra il 1875 e il 1884, in base ai progetti di Miklós Ybl, in stile neorinascimentale. Dal tempo della sua inaugurazione è il centro della vita musicale ungherese.

Opera House, interior. The three storeyed horse-shoe shaped auditorium is the most splendid part of the building. The frescoe on the ceiling is a masterpiece of Károly Lotz.

Innenraum der Budapester Oper. Der hufeisenförmige, dreistöckige Zuschauerraum ist der repräsentativste Teil des Gebäundes. Das Deckenfresko ist das Werk von Károly Lotz.

Interno del Teatro dell'Opera. Il semicerchio della platea e i tre piani di palchi sono la parte più rappresentativa dell'edificio. Il soffitto è decorato con un dipinto di grandi dimensioni di Károly Lotz.

 Synagogue in Dohány street. Designed by Lajos Förster and completed between 1854 and 1859 this Byzantine-Moorish style edifice with ceramic tiled onion shaped domes presents a picturesqe sight in Budapest.

 Die Große Synagoge in der Dohány-Straße. Von Ludwig Förster geplant, 1854–1859 gebaut ist der Monumentalbau in byzantinisch-maurischem Stil mit Keramikornamenten und Zwiebelkuppeln ein interessanter Farbfleck der Hauptstadt.

 La Sinagoga in Via Dohány. I costruzione, progettata da Lajos Först e realizzata fra il 1854 e il 1859, con sua cupola a cipolla, ornata di ceram che, con il suo stile bizantino–moresco piacevole nota di colore di Budapest.

🇬🇧 The building of the former Postal Savings Bank now housing the Hungarian National Bank.
This building, incorporating Hungarian folklore motifs, was planned by Ödön Lechner. It has a distinctly Art Nouveau style and is lavishly ornamented with majolica.

🇩🇪 Die ehemalige Postsparkasse – heute das Zentralgebäude der Ungarischen Nationalbank. Das mit Majolika reich verzierte, charakteristische Jugendstilgebäude wurde mit Anwendung von ungarischen Volkskunstmotiven von Ödön Lechner entworfen.

🇮🇹 L'edificio dell'ex Cassa di risparmio delle Poste ospita oggi la Banca Nazionale Ungherese. È stato progettato da Ödön Lechner. Costruito in stile liberty è riccamente ornato con maioliche a base di motivi dell' arte popolare ungherese.

St Stephen's Church (Basilica). Largest church in Budapest, bearing the sings of the Classicist design of József Hild as well as the Eclectic plans of Miklós Ybl. The church was built between 1851 and 1905.

St.-Stephan–Basilika. Budapests größter Sakralbau wurde 1851–1905 im klassizistischen (Architekt József Hild) und eklektischen (Architekt Miklós Ybl) Stil gebaut.

La Basilica di Santo Stefano. La più grande chiesa di Budapest porta le tracce dei progetti classicheggianti di József Hild e di quelli ecclettici di Miklós Ybl. La costruzione è iniziata nel 1851 ed è terminata nel 1905.

 Basilica (St Stephen's Church).
Altar Patrona Hungariae adorned by paintings of Gyula Benczúr, depicting St Stephen offering his crown to the Virgin.

St.-Stephan–Basilika. Patrona–Hungariae–Altar mit dem Gemälde Gyula Benczúrs: Offertorium, Stephan der Heilige reicht der Jungfrau Maria die ungarische Krone.

 **La Basilica di Santo Stefano.**
Nell'altare Patrona Hungariae il dipinto di Gyula Benczúr raffigura Santo Stefano mentre offre la Corona alla Ss. Vergine.

 Mass in the Basilica. The white marble statue of Saint Stephen was sculpted by Alajos Stróbl.

Messe in der Basilika. Die aus weißem Marmor gefertigte Statue von Stephan dem Heiligen ist das Werk von Alajos Stróbl.

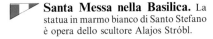 **Santa Messa nella Basilica.** La statua in marmo bianco di Santo Stefano è opera dello scultore Alajos Stróbl.

🇬🇧 CITY PARK

Favored recreation park of people of Budapest, seeking fresh air, amusements and relaxation. In can offer a bit of everything: artificial lake for rowing, parkland with high plane-trees, zoo and amusement park, but also museums, curious looking buildings and the most well known, a near symbolic square of the city – the Heroes' Square.

🇩🇪 STADTWÄLDCHEN

Hier finden die Budapester Erfrischung und Entspannung: auf dem künstlichen See, wo Boote zur Verfügung stehen, im Schatten der großen, alten Platanen, im Zoo oder im Luna Park. Hier gibt es Museen, verblüffende Baudenkmäler und eines der bekanntesten Wahrzeichen der ungarischen Hauptstadt, den Heldenplatz.

🇮🇹 IL PARCO COMUNALE

È il parco preferito dei budapestini desiderosi di aria fresca, di divertimento, di relax. Nel Városliget ognuno può trovare il tipo di svago che preferisce. C'è un lago in cui si può remare, un parco con grandi platani, un giardino zoologico e un Luna Park. Ma ci sono anche musei ed edifici stravaganti; si trova qui anche la Hősök tere, la Piazza degli Eroi che è ormai uno dei simboli che caratterizzano Budapest.

🇬🇧 **Millenary Monument.** The two arched colonna and the central column were erected to commemorate history of Hungary. Between the columns of the col nade stand statues of Hungarian rulers, kings and rei ing princes of Transylvania. The Monument was built the millenary celebrations.

Millenniumsdenkmal. Die aus zwei Viertelkreis-Säulenreihen und einer Gedenksäule bestehende Komposition ist der Geschichte Ungarns geweiht. Zwischen den Säulen stehen die Skulpturen ungarischer Führer, Könige und siebenbürgischer Fürsten. Das Denkmal wurde anläßlich der Millenniumsfeier der ungarischen Staates errichtet.

Il monumento del Millennio. Il monumento, a forma di semicerchio con colonnato e con una colonna centrale alta trentasei metri, rende omaggio alla storia dell'Ungheria. Tra le colonne si trovano le statue di condottieri, di re ungheresi e di principi transilvani. Il monumento è stato costruito in occasione del Millennio della fondazione dello Stato Ungherese.

43

 Museum of Fine Arts. This imposing building, built according to the plans of Albert Schickedanz in 1906, houses an impressive collection of old masters and modern art.

 Museum der Bildenden Künste. Eine der reichsten Kunstsammlungen Europas; nach Plänen von Albert Schikkedanz 1909 errichtet.

 **Il Museo delle Belle Arti.** L'imponente edificio realizzato nel 1906 in base ai disegni di Albert Schickedanz ospita una delle più ricche collezioni d'arte universale del mondo.

 Art Gallery. To the right of the Heroe's Square lies the Art Gallery, the largest exhibition hall in the country, an imposing building planned by Albert Schickedanz and Fülöp Herczog, commisioned by the Town Council to commemorate the millenary anniversary.

 Kunsthalle. Das imposante Gebäude mit antikisierender Fassade, das den Heldenplatz rechts abgegrenzt, ist Ungarns größter Ausstellungssaal. Mit dem Museum der Bildenden Künste an der gegenüberliegenden Seite des Platzes, wurde die Kunsthalle im Auftrag der Stadt, 1865 von Albert Schickedanz und löp Herczog errichtet.

 La Galleria dell'Arte. L'imponente edificio, con una facciata di stile greco antico, sul lato destro della Piazza degli Eroi è il più grande centro di esposizioni del Paese. Insieme al Museo delle Belle Arti è stata costruita da Albert Schickedanz e Fülöp Herczog su ordinazione del Comune che si preparava ai festeggiamenti del Millennio.

Raffaelo Santi: Madonna Esterházy. The small sized painting represents one of the most precious item in the important collection in the Museum of Fine Arts.

 Raffaello Santi: Esterházy-Madonna. Das kleinformatige Gemälde ist eines der wertvollsten Kunstwerke des Museums der Bildenden Künste.

 **Raffaello Santi: La Madonna Esterházy.** Il piccolo dipinto è uno dei pezzi più preziosi della prestigiosa collezione del Museo delle Belle Arti.

Vajdahunyad Castle. A group of buildings originally built for the Millenary Exhibition with the purpose to present the architectural history of Hungary.

Burg Vajdahunyad. Das Millennium Ungarns war das wichtigste Ereignis auch in der Geschichte des Stadtwäldchens. Für die Millenniumsausstellung wurde dieses besondere Bauwerk, das die Architekturgeschichte Ungarns zur Schau stellt, errichtet.

Il Castello di Vajdahunyad. Un insieme di costruzioni caratteristiche nello spazio del Parco Comunale illustra la storia dell'architettura ungherese. È stato messo a punto in occasione dell'Esposizione del Millennio.

Agricultural Museum

Landwirtschaftsmuseum

Il Museo dell'Agricoltura

Statue of Anonymus. Statue of the anonymous notary of Béla IV, who wrote the chronicle Gesta Hungarorum, was sculpted by Miklós Ligeti in 1903.

Statue des Chronisten Anonymus. Das Denkmal des namenlosen Notars von König Béla IV., des Verfassers der Gesta Hungarorum, errichtete Miklós Ligeti 1903.

La statua di Anonymus. La statua del cronista di re Béla IV, dell'autore del Gesta Hungarorum è opera dello scultore Miklós Ligeti e risale al 1903.

🇬🇧 BATHS OF BUDAPEST

No other metropolis of the world is so rich in thermal waters as is Budapest. People made use of it since centuries (see traces of an aquaduct leading from the Roman shore to Aquincum, or the Turkish baths left behind by the Turks.) Turn of the century has seen the shaping of a modern cult of baths by constructing baths named Császár and Lukács and the baths on Margaret Island. Széchenyi and Gellért baths completed the line.

DIE BÄDER VON BUDAPEST

Es gibt keine andere Hauptstadt der Welt, die so reich an Thermalquellen wäre wie Budapest. Ihre Einwohner nutzen seit Jahrhunderten die heilende Kraft dieser Quellen. (Siehe die Spuren des vom Römischen Ufer nach Aquincum führenden Aquaduktes oder die Dampfbäder aus der Türkenzeit.) Die moderne Badekultur nahm ihren Anfang mit dem Bau der Császár-, Margitszigeti- und Lukács-Bäder im 19. Jh. und erreichte ihren Höhepunkt mit der Eröffnung der Széchenyi- und Gellért-Bäder.

I BAGNI DI BUDAPEST

Non c'è un'altra capitale del mondo come Budapest che sia così ricca di acque termali. I suoi abitanti già da molti secoli si servono dell'acqua calda delle numerose sorgenti. (Vedi le tracce dell'acquedotto che porta dalla Római part (Riva Romana) ad Aquincum, o i bagni a vapore dell'epoca della dominazione turca). Il moderno culto balneare è iniziato nel secolo scorso a Budapest con la costruzione dei bagni Császár, Lukács, di quelli dell'Isola Margherita ed ha raggiunto la massima intensità con i bagni Széchenyi e Gellért.

Király Baths. A rare example of baths left from the Turkish period, rebuilt in the last century, but carefully preserving the original pool.

 Király-Bad. Eines der wenigen, aus der Türkenzeit erhalten gebliebenen Bäder, im 19. Jh. umgebaut, das Becken ist original.

 Il bagno Király. Uno dei pochi bagni dell'epoca turca rimasti intatti, è stato rinnovato nel secolo scorso, mantenendo però la piscina originale.

 **Gellért Baths.** Magnificent spa and hotel built in 1918, restored with great care, a bubble bath built in it in 1927. Medicinal baths attached to the Hotel, complete with medical treatments.

Gellért-Bad. Der prunkvolle Kurbadkomplex mit Hotel wurde 1918, das Sprudel- und Wellenbad 1927 übergeben. Fachärztliche Betreuung, Kurbehandlung.

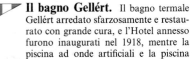 **Il bagno Gellért.** Il bagno termale Gellért arredato sfarzosamente e restaurato con grande cura, e l'Hotel annesso furono inaugurati nel 1918, mentre la piscina ad onde artificiali e la piscina coperta furono aggiunte nel 1927.

 Széchenyi Baths. Neo-Baroque Széchenyi medicinal baths is the greatest ornament of the City Park, fed by the hottest thermal spring of Europe.

 Széchenyi Bad. Das Széchenyi Kurbad ist ein Prachtbau des Stadtwäldchens. Die Quellen gehören zu den heißesten Thermalquellen in Europa.

Il bagno Széchenyi. È la gemma del Parco Comunale. Il bagno termale Széchenyi è alimentato da una delle più calde acque termali dell'Europa.

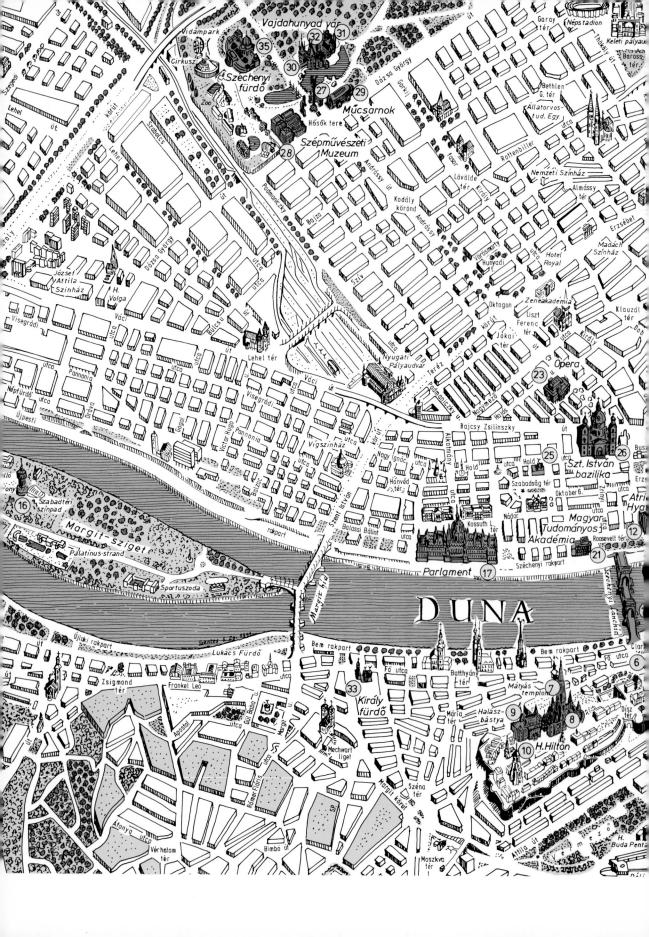

1. Statue of Bishop Gellért / Statue von Bischof Gellért / La statua del vescovo Gellért

2. Art Nouveau building in the Inner City / Jugendstil-Haus in der Innenstadt / Una casa in stile liberty nel Centro della città

3. Castle Palace and the southeastern walls / Das Burgschloß und die südöstlichen Burgmauern / Il Palazzo della Fortezza e le mura a sud-est

4. Castle Palace with the Mace Tower / Das Burgschloß mit dem Keulenturm / Il Palazzo della Fortezza con la Torre della Clava

5. King Matthias' Fountain / Matthiasbrunnen / La fontana di Mattia

6. Cable Railway / Die Standseilbahn / La funicolare

7. Matthias Church / Matthiaskirche / La Chiesa di Mattia

8. Statue of King St Stephen / Statue von König Stephan dem Heiligen / La statua di Re Santo Stefano

9. Fishermen's Bastion / Fischerbastei / Il Bastione dei Pescatori

10. Hilton Hotel – 11. Forum Hotel – 12. Atrium-Hyatt Hotel

13. Promenade / Donaukorso / Corso Danubio

14. Elisabeth Bridge / Elisabethbrücke / Il Ponte Elisabetta

15. Chain Bridge / Kettenbrücke / Il Ponte delle Catene

16. Water Tower on Margaret Island / Wasserturm auf der Margareteninsel / La Torre Idrica nell' Isola Margherita

17. Parliament / Parlament / Il Parlamento

18. Clotild Palaces / Klothilde-Paläste / Palazzi Klotild

19. Redoute / Die Pester Redoute / Il Ridotto

20. Váci street / Váci-Straße / La Via Váci

21. Academy of Sciences / Sitz der Ungarischen Akademie der Wissenschaften / L'Accademia Ungherese delle Scienze

22. Hungarian National Museum / Ungarisches Nationalmuseum / Il Museo Nazionale Ungherese

23. Opera House / Staatsoper / Il Teatro dell' Opera

24. Main Synagogue / Die Große Synagoge / La Sinagoga

25. Postal Savings Bank / Postsparkasse / La Cassa die Risparimio delle Poste

26. Basilica / St. Stephan-Basilika / La Basilica di Santo Stefano

27. Millenary Monument / Millenniumsdenkmal / Il monumento del Millenio

28. Museum of Fine Arts / Museum der Bildenden Künste / Il Museo delle Belle Arti

29. Art Gallery / Kunsthalle / La Galleria dell' Arte

30. Vajdahunyad Castle / Burg Vajdahunyad / Il Castello di Vajdahunyad

31. Agricultural Museum / Landwirtschaftsmuseum / Il Museo dell'Agricoltura

32. Statue of Anonymus / Statue des Chronisten Anonymus / La statua die Anonymus

33. Király baths / Király-Bad / Il Bagno Király

34. Gellért Baths / Gellért-Bad / Il Bagno Gellért

35. Széchenyi Baths / Széchenyi-Bad / Il bagno Széchenyi

Text by Ildikó Deák
Photos: Gábor Bérczi, Lóránt Bérczi,
Endre Domonkos, Csaba Gábler, Lajos Gál, Csaba Rafael,
Miklós Sehr, Zsolt Szabóky,
Károly Szelényi
Translation by Magdaléna Seleanu,
Zsuzsanna Lohn, Margit Dombai

ISBN 963 336 573-2
© Fine Arts Publishing House, Budapest 1991
Managing editor: Péter Látki
Design: Gyula Molnár
1573 9195